D1206441

NO FINISH LINE

LESSONS ON LIFE
AND CAREER

Meyer
Feldberg

COLUMBIA UNIVERSITY PRESS

NEW YORK

Columbia University Press
Publishers Since 1893
New York   Chichester, West Sussex
cup.columbia.edu

Copyright © 2020 Columbia University Press

Library of Congress Cataloging-in-Publication Data
Names: Feldberg, Meyer, author.
Title: No finish line : lessons on life and career / Meyer Feldberg.
Description: New York : Columbia University Press, [2020]
Identifiers: LCCN 2019058736 (print) | LCCN 2019058737 (ebook) |
ISBN 9780231196727 (hardcover) | ISBN 9780231551793 (ebook)
Subjects: LCSH: Feldberg, Meyer. | Business teachers—United States—
Biography. | Management—Study and teaching (Higher)—United States. |
Investment bankers—United States. | Conduct of life.
Classification: LCC HF1131 .F45 2020 (print) |
LCC HF1131 (ebook) | DDC 650.1—dc23
LC record available at https://lccn.loc.gov/2019058736
LC ebook record available at https://lccn.loc.gov/2019058737

Columbia University Press books are printed on
permanent and durable acid-free paper.

Printed in the United States of America

To my beloved wife, Barbara, whom I found sitting at a
swimming pool in Tel Aviv when she was eighteen, and to
our children, Lewis and Ilana, and our six grandchildren,
Sarah, Max, Noa, Adam, Danielle, and Sophia

In memory of my parents, Leon and Sarah,
and my sister, Abigail (Gaia)

CONTENTS

CONTENTS

CONTENTS

ACKNOWLEDGMENTS

I have lived on three continent, eight cities, studied at five Universities and been Dean of three and President of one.

1. Lady Luck. The right place at the right time.

2. Rudie Spoor, the Dutch swim coach who turned me into a world class butterfly swimmer at fifteen years old.

3. Columbia University, where I graduated in 1965 and came back as dean of the Business School in 1989, with a special thanks to President Lee Bollinger, who maintained my professorship and appointed me dean emeritus.

4. My life was greatly influenced by Milton Friedman, who was not only a great economist but a great friend.

5. Special thanks to Eric Schwartz and his team at Columbia University Press.

6. My early mentor Donald Jacobs, dean of the Kellogg School at Northwestern, also known as the Dean of Deans.

7. Great faculty at every institution, including Joseph E. Stiglitz, a Nobel Prize recipient who joined the faculty of Columbia Business School.

8. Michael Bloomberg, three-time mayor of New York City, who on the advice of his sister Marjorie Tiven appointed me president of NYC Global Partners.

9. Peter Martins, who brought me onto the board of the New York City Ballet.

10. My closest friend in New York, Russ Carson, whom I brought onto the Columbia Business School board of overseers and whose advice and friendship I've always relied on.

11. Safwan Masri, a colleague and great friend of mine and the entire Feldberg Family.

12. To the outstanding team of vice deans and associate deans. There are too many to mention, but they know who they are. I could not have been a success without them.

13. I would not have been able to complete this book without the extraordinary support of my executive assistant, Christina Borrero. She always offered excellent advice. Thank you, Christina.

14. I deeply acknowledge the love and support of my wife, Barbara, and my two children, Lewis and Ilana, as we moved around the world.

NO FINISH LINE

Meyer Feldberg, sixteen years old

LESSON 1

PACE YOURSELF

It was seven o'clock PM, the floodlights were on, the grandstand was packed, and the crowd roared. On your mark, get set, and *bang* sounded the starter's gun as eight swimmers dived into the pool for the hundred-meter butterfly championship in Johannesburg, South Africa. The year was 1959. One of those eight swimmers was me at age sixteen. I dived in, skimmed across the water. I felt like I was flying on top of it. I had never swum like this before. Toward the end of the first lap I saw that I was three lengths ahead of all the other swimmers. I turned at the wall and started swimming back ten meters, then twenty meters, then twenty-five meters. I was in a state of bliss. I was unstoppable, a record breaker in the making.

Then suddenly I felt a sharp pain. My legs and my arms didn't work. I dragged myself through the water with every muscle in my body aching, making it to the end of the pool barely two-tenths of a second ahead of the man who came in second. The whistle blew and I climbed from the pool and walked around to where my swim coach and the rest of the team were waiting. My teammates were uncomfortable and avoided eye contact, my coach angered and upset. He broke the tension and began shouting, "What happened? What did you do? What happened?" I shrugged and looked sheepishly at the floor. I didn't know what had happened. "When you made the turn, you were a second ahead of world record time," he continued, "and then in the middle of the second lap you slowed down. In the last quarter of the lap you simply collapsed! What happened?! What happened?!" Defeated in victory, I shook my head and walked away.

This race has haunted me for the last sixty-one years. In the end I failed. Sure, I won the race, but I was reckless and arrogant, too caught up in the feeling of success before I had earned it. My coach knew that, my teammates knew that, and years later I would come to know it, too.

At the age of fourteen I was an excellent swimmer, disciplined and determined. Every afternoon at four PM I went to the pool to train with a squad of a dozen young swimmers. I left home daily at five-thirty AM to train from six to eight, swimming a total of six thousand meters. Then I was off to school, and when school let out, I was back in the pool at four PM for another two hours and another six thousand meters, then home, dinner, and sleep, then wake up and do it all over again. There was only one indoor pool in the whole of Johannesburg back then, and it was thirty minutes

South African news clipping

away from home. It was not an option, so I swam in a 33.3-meter outdoor pool most of the year, seven days a week, even in the winter.

When I was fifteen I won the South African two-hundred-meter butterfly championship. South Africa in the 1950s was a small place, and the swim race was headline news: "15 Year Old School Boy Wins the 200 Meters Butterfly Event." I took swimming very seriously. It was my ticket to a wider world, and it paid off. Overnight, I became a visible athlete in a country that was and remains a fanatically sports-oriented nation. I was one of the youngest male "Springboks" in swimming history, representing South Africa at international events—all sports in South Africa are awarded a Springbok (deer) as a symbol of the national team. I wore a Springbok badge and a Springbok blazer, which were invitations to autograph seekers. During my teen years, it was a big deal, a very big deal. The visibility was extraordinary, and in retrospect, it was more than I knew how to handle.

The intensity and demands of four hours of swimming daily, up and down, staring at the "black line" at the bottom of the pool, enabled me as a young man to learn to be exceptionally focused. I carried this through my life, and I have had, by any measure, a successful life and a successful career. I swam competitively until I was eighteen and then quit, as there was no future in the sport. Apartheid South Africa was an international pariah, banned in 1962 from the 1964 Tokyo Olympic Games by the International Olympic Committee. I attended the University of Witwatersrand for a BA, Columbia Business School for an MBA, and the University of Cape Town back in South Africa for my PhD. On a visit to my sister in Israel I met Barbara, an English woman on holiday with her parents. She was eighteen, and I was twenty-one. We started talking together at a hotel swimming pool, and next thing I knew we had dinner that night and for the next four nights before she went back to London. A little over a year later we were married in New York and then again in London, and we've been constant companions ever since. We spent two years in Akron, where I worked for

4

BF Goodrich, before we moved back to South Africa and the University of Cape Town, for what would be the start of my long career in academia. While I was a lecturer at Cape Town I had visiting and teaching opportunities at MIT, Northwestern, Cranfield, and INSEAD. Through a close friend I became director of the Allen Center at Northwestern, a program focused on the burgeoning sector of executive education. Three years later I was dean of the Business School at Tulane University; five years later, president of the Illinois Institute of Technology. When Columbia Business School recruited me to reinvigorate its program I jumped at the opportunity, a role I held for fifteen years, and at the end of my third five-year term I retired as dean emeritus and joined Morgan Stanley as a senior advisor. Throughout I served as a member of the board of directors of numerous corporations and cultural institutions.

You can't plan your life. It's not a race. There is no finish line. There is a lot of luck involved in how you start and all that happens along the way. That said, just as Tolstoy begins *Anna Karenina* with the line "all happy families are alike," I believe that all successful people—or people who perceive themselves to be successful—are, more or less, alike. In the chapters that follow, using personal and professional life experience, I will model behavior that I think is representative of what it takes to be successful in the hope that you can learn what you may already know. Most of these lessons will seem like little more than common sense, but as with most things worthwhile, it's easier said than done. Success requires discipline, with attention to action above outcome. Not pacing myself in the hundred-meter butterfly race all those years ago is still meaningful to me today because I was emotionally undisciplined and could have failed for it. Pacing oneself is as critical in a swimming race as it is over a lifetime. Rather than just diving in and assuming that I could charge headlong through two laps, I should have paced myself. It turns out that in all aspects of life, pacing oneself matters.

LESSON 2

===

BE SELF-AWARE

It's eight AM, and I'm shouting at the family that we have to leave immediately. The slopes open at eight-thirty AM. We're behind schedule. Everyone piles into the Jeep, and we drive from our home to the main parking lot in Vail, which takes twelve minutes. We park. Everybody jumps out of the car. We take the skis off the roof, put them on our shoulders, hold the poles, and walk in our boots for ten minutes to the gondola. There is already a line, but I'm very pleased with myself. We're going to get the most out of the day. After a few minutes we walk into the gondola station, put our skis into the outside slots of the gondola, and clamber into the gondola with our poles. Fifteen minutes later, we are at the top of the mountain. My wife, Barbara, our fifteen-year-old son, Lewis, and our thirteen-year-old daughter, Ilana, have lifted their skis out of the outside slots and are carrying them together onto the snow at

Family skiing in Vail, Colorado

the top of the mountain, a breathless 12,000 feet above sea level.

Skiing is exhilarating on the way down, but the process of getting to the top of the mountain is exhausting. The children are grumpy. "Why do we have to be here so early?" asked Ilana. Because I am a lunatic. I have to be at the slopes when the lift line opens and at the end of the day when it closes at four PM. I need to be there at the last minute so I can sneak under the rope for a final bonus run. When the ski day ends and we retrace our steps, awkwardly carrying all of our gear from the mountain to the car, I'm not done. No, it is now time for me to put on my sneakers and drive to the gym. That's right, the gym.

When I get to the gym, I get changed, go to the floor and stretch, and then lift some weights. After half an hour, I go to the sauna for thirty minutes, then shower, get dressed, and drive home to meet the family for dinner. It's a long, long day with almost zero down time, but I can't have it any other way. The rest of my family and our friends who stay with us during ski season don't appreciate my compulsiveness. They've given me an odious nickname, which I will not disclose.

Fast forward forty years, and we're still skiing about thirty days a year, now with six grandchildren in tow. We leave the house at nine AM, rather than eight AM. We take a break for lunch. We end the ski day at three PM, not four PM. I go home for a rest before dinner. Age has not completely changed my compulsive behavior, and I have continued my maniacal ski day into my late seventies—but stamina, it turns out, is finite.

The next day I am back in New York. It's eight-thirty AM, and I have an all-day board meeting ahead of me, followed by a dinner with clients. I get out of bed and drink two cups of coffee, eat yogurt, and then spend thirty minutes on stretching and abdominal exercises. I shower, get dressed, and walk to the board meeting. I walk everywhere. By the time I arrive home from a full, exhausting day, I check my pedometer and find that on top of everything else, I've walked six miles.

I work out every day. The only day I don't work out is if I'm in the air on a long-haul flight. Every morning I spend thirty minutes on stretching and abdominal exercises. I go to the gym seven days a week. I ride a stationary bicycle three times a week. I lift weights four times a week. Every day, day in and day out, no matter what.

This is not all. The first thing I do when I get up in the morning is get on the scale and weigh myself. When I get home in the evening, I weigh myself. After dinner, I weigh myself. My compulsiveness with my weight knows no bounds. If I walk past a store and see a scale in the window, I'll walk in and weigh myself. This is not normal behavior, and I know that, but I also know where it comes from.

When I was eighteen and at the peak of my swimming career, I weighed 152 pounds. After South Africa was banned from the Olympics, I stopped swimming. I don't mean to say that I swam less—I stopped swimming altogether. I went from an intensive two six-thousand-yard training sessions a day to zero. In order to swim 12,000 yards a day I had to consume five thousand to six thousand calories per day. When I stopped swimming, I continued eating like a swimmer, and my weight ballooned to an unhealthy two hundred pounds. This put a scare into me, which I haven't been able to shake for fifty years. I've spent the decades watching my diet and my weight and exercising relentlessly.

In recent years, I've slowed down. I pace myself, and I have become more self-aware of the effect that my relentlessness can have on my friends, colleagues, family, and myself. I no longer go to every dinner I am invited to. I no longer travel to every city when called on by friends or alumni or clients to visit. When I do travel, I plan for downtime; Barbara joins me everywhere I go. My family and friends think I still have a long way to go, and they're right. I'm not ready to retire, but I have also come to terms with the fact that I'm no longer a teenager diving into a swimming pool for a two-hundred-meter butterfly race, and I no longer expect my friends, family, and colleagues to keep up with that teenager or to share his obsessive habits.

I have become reflective and self-aware. There are things I haven't done that I would still like to do, and there are things that I've done that I now know I should not have done and wished I hadn't. In the end, I can say without qualification that self-awareness is a key to success. It unlocks our hidden motivations and explains why we do what we do. Self-awareness helps us understand how our behaviors affect ourselves and others. It is through self-awareness that we treat ourselves and others with the respect we all deserve.

LESSON 3

═══════════

TAKE RISKS TO FIND
THE RIGHT FIT

Opportunities arise at unexpected times and in unexpected places. There's no way to know what will work out. Which career move is right? Is this move happening at the right time? You just don't know. What you do know, however, is that if you want your career to progress, when an opportunity arises that you feel can move you toward your goal, you need to trust your intuition and go for it. This is precisely what happened to me when I became dean of Columbia Business School. My path back to Columbia Business School was indirect and would not have been possible without a few chances taken and chance occurrences along the way.

In late 1972, I traveled to New Orleans for the annual, three-day Worldwide Meeting of Business School Deans. This was the first time I was attending the event, as the new dean of the University of Cape Town Business School. On my second evening in New Orleans, I thought I'd treat myself to an authentic Creole experience, so I walked over to the internationally famous Court of the Two Sisters restaurant, on Royal Street in the heart of the French Quarter. There is limited opportunity for downtime at an academic conference, so I decided on an early booking and looked forward to some time alone in the restaurant's lovely courtyard.

I was halfway through my meal and enjoying the quietude when a woman came up to me and said, "My husband and I see you dining by yourself; would you like to join us?" I was caught off guard but flattered by the invitation, and fifteen minutes later I was sitting at their table for coffee. They introduced themselves as Bob and Audrey Pritzker; they were from Chicago and visiting New Orleans for business. We had an enjoyable conversation and said our goodbyes. I went back to the hotel and thought nothing further of it for the rest of my trip.

Sometime later, back in my office in Cape Town, I was flipping through the *Wall Street Journal* when I noticed a small headline announcing the death of someone named Donny Pritzker. The name was familiar, and it struck me that Donny must be related to the couple I'd met in New Orleans. I sent a condolence note to the Pritzkers, mentioned that I was going to be in Chicago in November on a faculty recruiting trip, and suggested that we meet again. I received a prompt reply and, to my surprise, an invitation to stay with them for a couple of days at their apartment.

I arrived in Chicago a couple of months later and headed straight to my first round of appointments at the University of Chicago, then as now world renowned as a leader in the field of economics. I spent the morning with Dick Rosett, the dean of the Business School, discussing possible visiting professors. When it was time for lunch, we crossed the campus to the faculty club, and he gave me a tour along the way. He asked where I was going to be staying that evening, and I mentioned that I was staying with a nice couple I met in New Orleans, the Pritzkers. "Oh," he said, "that's nice." We continued walking toward the Quadrangle Club, and on the way he stopped and pointed to a complex of magnificent buildings. He put his hand on my arm and said, "You see those buildings over there? That's the Pritzker School of Medicine." I stopped and asked, "My Pritzkers?" He replied, "Yes, your Pritzkers." The dean suggested that I come to his home for a drink at five o'clock and that he would arrange for a car to take me from there to the Pritzkers' apartment.

We spent a pleasant hour together before the car arrived. When I got into the car there was another gentleman already sitting in the backseat who was also going to the Pritzkers' for dinner. I introduced myself and mentioned that I was visiting from Cape Town on a recruiting trip. He knew a lot about the University of Chicago, so I asked if he worked there. "Yes," he said, with a twinkle in his eyes. "I'm the president." I was barely thirty and was finding this all a bit surreal, a far cry from South Africa. The evening continued on into a formal dinner party attended by a number of Chicago power brokers. After dinner, I went to my suite to get ready for bed to find that my suitcase had been unpacked and my clothing pressed and hung up. I stayed with the Pritzkers for two evenings before I left for the West Coast to visit Stanford and Berkeley. Who would have thought that the nice couple who had invited me to join them for coffee belonged to one of the wealthiest and most powerful families in Chicago?

In 1978, an opportunity arose through the dean of Northwestern's business school to become the director of the Allan Center and head of Executive Education. I accepted the position and moved permanently from South Africa to the United States. I was at Northwestern for two and a half years; we then left for New Orleans, where I had been appointed dean of the Graduate School of Business at Tulane University. One of my first tasks at Tulane was to create a Board of Overseers for the business school, and one of the first people I invited to join the board was Bob Pritzker. He accepted and attended at least two or three of the meetings a year for the next five years. During the fourth year of my deanship, Bob, who was also the co-chairman of the Board of Trustees of the Illinois Institute of Technology, persuaded me to leave Tulane and New Orleans and move back to Chicago as president of IIT.

I was ready to leave Tulane for a new opportunity as a university president. I wanted something bigger. It was time to take another risk. Still, Barbara and I were sad to leave New Orleans—we had developed many close friendships during our five years there—but this was a presidency, and careerwise

SUNDAY TIMES, November 26, 1978

Whizkid Professor Feldberg quits for US post

By NIC VAN OUDTSHOORN

Prof Meyer Feldberg ...
"a great challenge"

PROFESSOR Meyer Feldberg, 36, director of the Graduate School of Business at the University of Cape Town, will leave South Africa next April to take up a top academic position in the United States.

Professor Feldberg — who at 29 was the youngest professor at UCT — has been appointed director of the Centre for Executive and Management Education at Northwestern University in Chicago.

Not political

He said his decision to leave South Africa was "purely professional" and had nothing to do with politics.

He had resigned from his post at UCT with mixed feelings.

"Northwestern University is constructing a major new centre for executive and management education.

"This new centre will be completed next September and I have been invited to be its first director."

Professor Feldberg said the decision to accept this position was taken after much soul-searching.

He had been at the Graduate School of Business at UCT for 11 years, seven of them as director.

He now felt it essential for his personal growth and development to seek a new challenge.

"Northwestern Graduate School of Management has for five years been ranked as one of the top 12 schools in the United States, and is ranked number seven.

"The school has an academic faculty of more than 90, including many world-famous scholars.

"The opportunity to work with a large and illustrious faculty in developing a major international centre for management education will be a great challenge."

Professor Feldberg said he would continue as a director, of the Graduate School of Business at UCT until he left South Africa.

He has a remarkable success record.

At 15 he gained Springbok swimming colours and was the youngest Springbok in the contingent to the Commonwealth Games in 1958.

He was one of the youngest MBA graduates at Columbia University in the United States, then became the youngest full professor at UCT and later the youngest director of the Graduate School of business.

South African news clipping

this was a step up to a new level and an incredible learning opportunity. My three years at IIT were a complete change. At the time, the university was primarily a school of engineering, science, and architecture. I learned a great deal about these disciplines during my three years as president, but the fit just wasn't there. I had taken a chance. There is always a risk that things don't work out.

Late in my third year at ITT, I was sitting in my office when I heard a knock at the door. My assistant said there was a man outside who wanted to see me. It was Ben Rosen, a member of the Board of Overseers I had composed at Tulane. He had not called or asked for an appointment; it was a pleasant surprise. We sat down at my conference table and talked about our respective lives and families, and he reminded me of the good times we'd had at Tulane. After half an hour he looked at me and dropped the news: "Columbia Business School is looking for a new dean," he said, "and I would like your advice. I am the chairman of the search committee."

We went through a number of names of potential candidates and discussed what kind of dean Columbia was looking for. Then, he looked at me and said, "Actually, the search committee has already made a decision, and I have forwarded it to the president of the university. We are all agreed that you should be and are going to be the new dean." I remained quiet. "I've only been here for three years," I said. "I can't leave just yet." "That can't be helped," he replied. "You are a Columbia graduate, the school needs a new dean, and you are the perfect match." I knew he was right and that IIT wasn't the right place for me. I felt a great deal of angst over the next couple of months as Barbara and I made the decision for me to resign as president of IIT. I knew that this would not go over well in Chicago, but the opportunity to move back to New York, where we had first lived before we were married, was irresistible.

Timing matters. It was time to take another risk. You need to know when it's time to move on. When you need to move to a different position. A different firm. A different university. A different city. The biggest risk that we run is that we hesitate. We are fearful of moving to a new place. We kick the can down the road. The opportunity is lost. We now have the problem of not being comfortable where we are but have lost the opportunity to go elsewhere. How often do we say "Let's wait awhile, we'll stay where we are for another couple of years and then move"? In the meantime, an opportunity has gone by. To build a great career, an exciting career, a rewarding career, we must avoid dead ends.

As I had anticipated, my resignation as president of IIT created a huge storm across the campus and among the faculty. People claimed that I was deserting the institution after only three years and at a critical time—and they weren't wrong. The co-chair of the board committee was incensed. He called to say he was sending his car to bring me to his office to explain why my decision was unacceptable. We had a contentious thirty-minute discussion before I left his office on the way back to IIT. I called Bob Pritzker and told him about my decision and about my meeting with his colleague. Bob and I had been close friends for a long time now. He was extremely unhappy about my decision but not hostile. He understood the risk I had taken to come to IIT and why it made sense for me to follow this new opportunity back to Columbia and New York.

I had told the co-chair that I would get back to him after speaking to Pritzker. It was late on a Friday afternoon, and he did not want to talk to me on the telephone. He insisted on having a meeting with me and Pritzker the next morning, a Saturday. We met at the O'Hare Hyatt at eight o'clock in the morning, in an empty, dreary coffee shop. I sat on one side of the table, Pritzker and his colleague on the other. The latter did all the talking. He shook his finger in my face and said, "Young man, it is your destiny to remain as president of IIT." I was speechless. Pritzker didn't say a word. I looked at his finger and said, "I'm forty-eight. I'm not a young man. And you do not control my destiny." It was clear that he didn't get me, didn't understand why ITT didn't work, and couldn't see why it was best for me to return to New York. He glared at me and announced, "As of this moment you are no longer president of IIT. I am taking over as chief executive officer of the university." He then stood and walked out of the coffee shop. Bob Pritzker and I just stared at each other. I recognized a kindness in his look, which I remembered from that first time we met, in New Orleans at the Court of the Two Sisters. "I'll drive you home," he said. We got into his car, a practical old-model station wagon, and on

Barbara Feldberg, Bob and Irene Pritzker

the way back to my apartment he told me he was "sorry that it ended so badly."

It is important to note that Bob Pritzker and his co-chairman were certainly among the most powerful and important people not only in Chicago but in the United States. The other co-chairman of the board was Bob Galvin, the chairman, CEO, and controlling shareholder of Motorola. He personally called the president of Columbia University to complain about attracting me away from IIT. The president of Columbia and I spoke, and he asked me to be very sure that I could make this work. As it turned out, during my third year at Columbia as dean, I invited Bob to visit me and give a lecture to the student body. The event was a huge success. The students gave Galvin a standing ovation, and at that point he and I both walked to the center of the auditorium and shook hands. At that coffee shop in O'Hare, who would have thought this could possibly ever happen?

Three years ago, my wife and I were invited to the inauguration of a new president of IIT. I was one of the two guest speakers on the occasion. We can see that there's another lesson that comes out of this chapter. Don't burn bridges. Reach out those who feel that you have behaved badly. Make your peace. Life is short.

Bob Pritzker and I remained close friends until he passed away in 2011. I left for New York shortly after the events at IIT and haven't looked back. Leaving IIT felt like a big risk, but, in retrospect, it wasn't much of a risk at all. I had learned where I belonged. I started at Columbia as a student in 1963 and returned as dean in 1989, and I remained dean for three five-year terms, until 2004. More on all of that comes later. When I arrived at Columbia I immediately began creating a Board of Overseers. The first person I asked to join the board and serve as chairman was Ben Rosen. Of course, he had no option.

LESSON 4

LIFE IS FRAGILE

My father, Leon, had his first heart attack in our home in Johannesburg back in 1954. I was twelve years old. I got out of bed early in the morning at around six-thirty AM, just like any other day, and I began walking to the staircase to go downstairs for breakfast. I passed my parents room, glanced inside, and got a shock. There were people in the room other than my mother, who was still in her dressing gown. My father was lying in the bed, a doctor with a black bag hovering over him. My sister, Gaia, was upset and had her arms around our mother, Sarah. How I hadn't been woken up by what had clearly transpired, I cannot say.

Before I even entered the room, I could tell that something scary and bad had happened. The doctor took me aside and told me my father had had a heart attack. "But he will be alright?" I asked. The extremely dour physician said he didn't know. He told me that I should stay home from school that day. "Your father is very sick," he said. "He can't be, we're all going to the game reserve this week. For ten days," I said in youthful disbelief and innocence and with increasing fear. My mother and sister saw this and put their arms around me. I looked at my father lying on his back with his eyes closed: this was the first time in my twelve years of life that I felt a truly existential panic.

My dad was the most energetic man I knew and the center of my world. He was the kind of guy that stood out at every party, in the center of the room, telling stories, cracking jokes, making friends. The man I saw there lying on the bed with his eyes closed in a darkened room simply could not be my father. It was obviously him, but my vibrant and amazing dad was missing. My older sister, aware that I was having difficulty taking this all in, walked me downstairs to have something to eat and calm my panic. We waited for a specialist to arrive, a doctor reputed to be the best cardiologist in Johannesburg.

After a brief breakfast, I walked outside into the garden to try to gather myself and come to grips with what was happening. My life to that point had been idyllic. I hadn't had a care in the world and was not remotely self-reflective about just how well-off I was. What would happen now that my father was so sick? Would all of that change? We lived in a large, beautiful home with a lush garden and a swimming pool. We had a black 1954 Buick, not a common car in South

Family photo

Africa at the time. We had two maids and a gardener on staff. I think back and realize that this was the first emotional crisis of my life. I did not understand this at the time, but as I reflect back, I realize that I was in no way prepared to lose my father. Lost in thought, standing alone on the patio of our garden, my uncle, my mother's brother, walked out of the sliding doors. He came up to me and said, "So are you worried about your father? You know he could die." He smiled as he said that, and I wanted to hit him with every ounce of my being. I probably should have, but I didn't. This was more than sixty years ago, and I still remember that smirk and that moment vividly.

For the next three months, all of our family life focused on caring for my father. Back in those days, heart attack patients were expected to lie in bed for weeks as part of their recovery. Why this was so I still don't know. They were not allowed to walk up or down stairs or do anything that exerted energy. They simply had to lie in bed, so that is what he did. I had never seen my father this way. During his convalescence at home, he was allowed to have friends and colleagues from his business visit him. When this happened he perked up, and I saw him returning, albeit slowly, to his old self. Eventually he recovered completely and went back to work as editor of the *South African Jewish Times*.

For me it was a blurry but immense emotional experience to realize that my father was ill and could die. It was at this point that I first learned that life is fragile and that you must make the most of the time you have while you still have it. This is a lesson that, sadly, cannot be unlearned. All these years later I recognize what an enormous amount of emotional energy was required for me to get through those first three months of my dad's recovery. This was his first heart attack but not his last, and I knew that even once he recovered, something like this was bound to happen again, at any time. It was out of our control. I was emotionally fragile for many years because of this, and every time I came home from school or an evening out, or if I saw an ambulance or heard its siren, I would panic in fear of seeing my dad lying lifeless on the bed.

My father had several heart attacks before the fatal one, which happened in Israel in 1968. Barbara, our son, Lewis, our daughter, Ilana, and I were all in Evanston, Illinois, where I was teaching at Northwestern. I remember coming home from a conference, and before I could even get to our apartment Barbara cracked open the door and looked at me. I knew what that look meant. It was the moment I had dreaded but always knew was coming sooner or later. "Dad?" I said. "Yes," she nodded. The four of us flew the next day to Tel Aviv for the funeral, where Lewis Rabinowitz, the former chief rabbi of South Africa and dad's oldest friend, officiated at the gravesite.

After my father's funeral, my mother remained in Tel Aviv, living a couple of blocks away from my sister, Gaia, her husband, Yerach, and their three children. She came to visit us a couple of times in Evanston, but on her last visit it was clear that my mother was seriously ill. My mother was the rock of my life. She was an exceptionally well-educated person who had attended university in South Africa and graduated with a master's degree in the 1930s. This was unheard of at the time. She was a classics scholar who read and understood ancient Greek and could read, write, and speak Latin. I recall being with my parents in Italy, where she spoke to the Italians in Latin, which, though the root language of Italian, few Italians would hear outside of a pre–Vatican II mass. She died of cancer in my sister's home in 1998. I flew to Israel three or four times to visit her that year. Life is fragile, and I wanted to make sure we made the most of what was left.

My mother was seventy-two when she died, as was my father when he passed away. When she was seventy-two, my beloved sister became ill and died of cancer. This is a family tradition I have thankfully avoided. Barbara and I had visited with Gaia several times before her death, and we were called back a couple of days before she died in the hospital in Tel Aviv. Both our children came with us, and I have a vivid memory of being in Gaia's hospital room with Barbara, Lewis, and Ilana looking at my sister, who was at death's door. Emotionally I was brought right back to that morning when I was twelve. Lewis and I were standing on opposite sides of the bed, and I looked up and saw him weeping. Was this his first experience of life's fragility? It was all too much. Whenever Barbara and I visit Israel, the first thing we do is visit the graves of my parents and sister.

In 2014, Barbara and I flew to Los Angeles to attend the funeral of my friend Teddy. Teddy and I had met at the Saxonwald School when we were five years old. We went to nursery school, junior school, high school, and college together. We were like family. Barbara and I arrived in Los Angeles just in time for the funeral, at a cemetery across the mountains facing the Ronald Reagan Presidential Library in Simi Valley. I stood in silent sadness during the ceremony, remembering the more than sixty-five years Teddy and I had spent together in Johannesburg and in the United States. Barbara and I had visited with Teddy about six months before his funeral. We sat on the patio of a restaurant having lunch together; I helped Teddy cut his food. Barbara and I left the lunch to return to New York and did not say anything to each other until we were on the plane. She looked at me and said, "You know we will be going back again soon." I knew and hung my head in sadness.

The loss of family and friends is painful. It requires fortitude and must be confronted. Over the years I have learned that our loved ones are always around us. I don't think that I go through a week without thinking about my parents or my sister. It doesn't hurt that Barbara is an artist and that in every room of our apartment hang paintings that remind me of my family. I see them every day, in every room, and they always bring me back to wonderful memories. We talk about my parents and my sister every week; sometimes every day. Life is fragile, but the memories of our loved ones aren't. The dreams and visions of family and friends are always with us. So long as we keep them close to us, they will never go away.

LESSON 5

ADMIT YOUR MISTAKES

Children are adaptable, but only so much. Our son, Lewis, and our daughter, Ilana, were both born in Cape Town. We were fortunate in that we had a large house and that my parents would visit us from Johannesburg for long periods of time. During my early years as the dean of the University of Cape Town Business School I was like most ambitious young men. I was always in a hurry for the next accomplishment. I let my career take center stage. I missed important moments in the lives of my children. This was a mistake.

At the time I was blinkered by ambition and thought I was doing the right thing for myself and for my family. I was building a business school. I was teaching multiple classes of MBAs and executive MBAs. At least once or twice a month I would start an executive program at five PM on a Sunday evening and not return home until nine PM. My parenting skills were limited, as was my time at home. I assumed that Barbara could take care of the children and that my parents would be around to help her. My father walked seven-year-old Lewis to the school bus each morning when he visited. I rushed in and out of the house during the week, and if there was a problem, I would shout out as I walked out the door, "Don't worry, Dad will fix it when he comes back from taking the kids to Hebrew school." We sometimes had to wait three months for my parents to visit us before a light bulb would get changed.

As I reflect on these early years in Cape Town, I realize that I was an inattentive parent who relied on Barbara and my parents to take care of the house and the children while I built my career. When we left Cape Town for Chicago, things took a radical turn. There was no family to rely on, and while I did have friends and associates in Chicago, the children and Barbara did not. My friends in Chicago were good friends, but they had their own lives and children and certainly could not help out with ours. Barbara and I only had each other.

It was only at this point that I realized that my life was not entirely about me but about the family unit that had moved eight thousand miles to a new continent, a new country, a new city, and a new life. It was exciting but also very challenging, especially for Barbara and the kids. We moved for my opportunity. Overnight I realized that the family was paramount and that I had to be involved not only in my own life and career but in the lives of the three other people who saw me as their protector.

In hindsight, I didn't consider that it would take a substantial amount of time for the kids to adjust to this new world. It is a fallacy to think that young people adjust quickly and easily. My kids didn't have any friends. Their classroom atmosphere was different. Their school hours and assignments were different. Not considering my kids was a mistake. It took me a while, but I now understand it is difficult for children to adjust to new cities and new schools. Children do not quickly figure out how to fit into a new environment. Parents should anticipate before the move that there will be ups and downs and awkward moments. Moving to a new continent, country, and city is complicated for parents, and it is a time when children simply must be central in your life.

LESSON 6

CONFRONT INJUSTICE

Injustice is something that is frequently understood in the abstract, unless one is the victim of it. I grew up in South Africa under apartheid, the formal government policy of segregation and white supremacy. I benefited from that system by nature of being white. But I am also Jewish, which puts me at something of a distance from the Afrikaners, the descendants of the Dutch, German, and French settlers. Rather, I was part of an at times insular minority. Nevertheless, apartheid was a way of life that I was born into. As a child I was thoughtless about it in the way that children are. But now I was back in South Africa as an adult, with a family of my own. I had lived in the United States, which had and still has problems of segregation and discrimination. I had a position of influence within the University of Cape Town, and this meant there were opportunities to confront injustice head on and take a different path. One can and should use one's power to do the right thing.

Barbara and I moved to South Africa from Akron, Ohio, in 1968. My wife had never visited South Africa. We began our life as a married couple looking to build a family and a life. We bought a small house in a pleasant suburb about two miles from Cape Town. Our two children, Lewis and Ilana, were born there. In spite of its limited space, it was never just us and the kids. Both my parents and Barbara's mother stayed with us for months at a time to "meet" the children. We got two dogs. Two large dogs. Kleintjie was a mix between an Alsatian and a Great Dane, and Bella was an adorable and friendly Labrador. We lived happily and crowded in that house for three years, and then with the aid of my late father, we purchased a larger house in the Kenilworth suburb of Cape Town. The house had a big, beautiful garden, a swimming pool, and a sauna. We had plenty of space for the kids, the pets, and our extended family.

Our early years back in Cape Town were exceptionally carefree. It was a complete change in lifestyle from what we had in Ohio. Cape Town is a warm coastal city on two oceans, the Atlantic and the Indian. During the summer we often went to the beach. Both our kids attended the same Jewish day school, and when they weren't at school, they were in the pool. We rapidly built a large network of wonderful friends; there were parties to host or attend seemingly every week. Our young daughter became close friends with a girl who lived next door, and a ladder was placed against the shared garden wall so that they could climb over and play together.

My commute to the university was a mere fifteen-minute drive. And what a drive it was! The route was a beautiful trip through the mountains with a view of the ocean. I drove my red Corvair, shipped from the States as part of our move. It was a fun car and probably the only one of its kind in the country. It was no Ferrari, but I was ogled wherever I went. When I got to work I was very engaged at the University of Cape Town as dean of the Business School and dean of the Faculty of Commerce. Moving from a faculty position to administration was a big deal for me professionally and opened me up to a new level of organizational responsibility, leadership, and engagement with the wider world. I was now a representative of the university and all it stood for. I traveled the world recruiting faculty to come and teach at the school. The University of Cape Town Business School grew and flourished, aided by the network of colleagues I had built in the United States as a student and professor. It was probably the best business school on the continent of Africa. The quality of students was excellent. They were serious and engaged, as were their instructors.

But looming behind my idyllic home life and career was a dark side: the role apartheid played in all aspects of public life in South Africa. Being dean of the University of Cape Town Business School was a big deal, and I was more of a public figure than I had been in past roles. People knew who

I was. I was publicly responsible for the actions of the Graduate School of Business and responsible to the faculty, staff, and students. Any action I took was imbued with symbolic meaning.

The atmosphere in the country and city and at the university was starting to change, however. A movement had developed in the United States seeking to disallow U.S. companies from either investing or doing business in South Africa. This divestment movement, together with the banning of South African athletes and sports teams from international events, was eventually to lead to the breakdown of apartheid. It was a wake-up call to many whites in South Africa to take action.

The University of Cape Town was essentially a white university. The graduate school of business was completely white. There were no black Africans. There were no Indians. There were no students of mixed race. In 1974, I could no longer be complicit in the apartheid system and determined to break what was government policy and confront injustice where I saw it, and in a public fashion. At that time, South Africa had two ministers of education. One was for the white population and the other was for black affairs. I had for a couple of years invited black South Africans to come to speak at the university. This was always a touchy issue. Lucas Mangope, from Bophuthatswana, was one of the first African chiefs to speak at the business school. He was the leader of what was known as a Bantu Homeland, which was an area designated by the white government as a territory for a particular tribe, which allowed for some degree of authority and self-management. The second black leader was Gatcha Buthelezi. He was at the time the chief of the Zulus. The Zulus were and remain the largest of the tribal groups in South Africa. Gatcha Buthelezi and I established a close and warm relationship. During one of these visits to the campus, I asked him whether he could find a black Zulu who would be a suitable candidate for enrollment at the business school. He said he would get back to me.

A couple of months later, I flew to Durban, a city that bordered the homelands known as Kwa-Zulu. I stayed at the Edward Hotel, an all-white hotel, and invited Chief Buthelezi for lunch. Both I and the hotel had to get permission for him

Gatsha Buthelezi in Durban

to be admitted to the building for lunch. This indignity was a small price to pay for what was part of a larger goal. Permission was ultimately granted, and we had lunch on the veranda of the hotel, overlooking the ocean. It became a big news event. Newspapers around the country published photographs of the two of us sitting on the veranda having lunch. There were visible security officials watching us eating. In South Africa at the time this sort of meeting simply didn't happen.

The lunch ended, and some months later Buthelezi called and told me he had a candidate for the University of Cape Town Business School. His name was Sam Zondi. His application came in, and he was admitted. I was, however, told by the Ministry of Education that we would need special permission for him to attend the business school. This permission process required me to pressure the minister of education to allow the University of Cape Town to admit Mr. Zondi into the business school, which I did. After some months, the ministry agreed, but with a proviso. Sam Zondi could not live on the campus. He would have to live in one of the "African/Colored townships" fifteen miles away. This was an attempt to break my support, but I wouldn't back down. Confront injustice where it lives.

Initially my colleagues and I made the decision that we would get him into the school and that after he was formerly admitted we would chip in and buy him a car so that he could drive back and forth between the township and the university. After a couple of weeks, I realized the absurdity of this

Sam Zondi...man behind the face of change

By JULIAN KRAFT

TIMES ARE a-changing. Sam Zondi, business development officer for Barclays Bank in Natal since the beginning of the year, is just one symbol of the changing pattern.

Mr Zondi, 37, has more than enough qualifications to perform his unique job. He has a B. Com from the University of Zululand and a Master of Business Administration degree from the University of Cape Town. He is believed to be the only African in South Africa with an MBA.

He got his present job after a spell of working for the KwaZulu Government in Maritzburg as an internal auditor, which carried the title of "financial inspector". He turned down an offer to become a "professional assistant" in the SA Bureau for Economic Research — an advisory body linked to the Bantu Development Corporation — to take his job.

The Barclays job offered more scope and a greater challenge for him. The Bureau for Economic Research job would have meant in effect, being a trainee economist for three years before being due for elevation to the post of economic advisor to the KwaZulu Government.

For Mr Zondi the training period is over. He wants to get into the mainstream of African business, where he believes he has a role to play in helping African businessmen to run and expand their businesses.

He would like to see African businesses develop into large viable units, getting away from the "sole ownership" pattern which exists at present in the townships and elsewhere. This could be done, he says, if African entrepreneurs formed partnerships and pooled their resources to develop one business together. They could even float their companies and offer shares to obtain the necessary funds for development.

"The Bantu Investment Corporation, by offering loans, definitely has a role to play in the development of African business, but I do not think the small man should lean too heavily on this kind of assistance. I'd like to see African business men become self-sufficient in their own community".

He also wants to discourage urban-based entrepreneurs from going into the homelands to set up business because of the restrictions on trading rights in the urban townships. They should stay put in spite of difficulties, he says. The restrictions and difficulties are not insurmountable.

"The urban areas are where the biggest markets are and where most of the money can be made," says Mr. Zondi.

His other piece of advice to African business men is: "They must recognise that they are in competition with White businesses for the African market although separate development appears to offer them protection by barring White business from operating in the Black areas.

"They must develop their businesses so that they can offer services, variety of goods and prices comparable with the businesses in the White areas."

In his job as business development officer for Barclays in Natal Mr. Zondi has four distinct functions:

● Improving contact between the bank and its African customers. This mainly involves clearing up misunderstandings and overcoming language difficulties.

● Business education, which up to now has meant giving instruction to African business men in bookkeeping. Mr. Zondi is also establishing links with the provincial and national African Chambers of Commerce with a view to furthering business education in the African community.

● Assisting with borrowing proposals, which involves checking credentials of Africans who have applied for financial assistance.

● Presenting bank services to the Africans, the majority of whom only use savings accounts at present. Mr. Zondi has had a good response from sophisticated Africans to use Barclaycard and is also trying to encourage people to use fixed deposits and take life insurance through the bank.

Mr. Zondi started studying for a B.Com. by correspondence through Unisa while he was employed as a clerk in the Department of Justice. He finished his degree at the University of Zululand. He got his MBA, which normally requires two years of study, in only one year, in 1972.

A new role in business . . . Sam Zondi

Sam Zondi

arrangement and simply allocated a dorm room on the campus for Sam Zondi. I did not request permission from the ministry; I simply went ahead and put him into the dorm. No students objected. I realize that this story must sound ridiculous to any sensible individual, but that's the way it was. The government knew what I had done but were forced to turn a blind eye so that the situation didn't become a larger political issue.

Systems of injustice like apartheid remain in place because people go along with them. They collapse through the cumulative efforts of people standing against them and doing their part where they can. You should recognize how and when you can stand against injustice in your own life. In January 2017, I visited the University of Cape Town's Graduate School of Business. Like all universities, much hasn't changed over the decades, but something had, something unimaginable in 1968. The new dean was a black African. More than 70 percent of the students were black Africans, Indians, or people of mixed race, what used to be referred to as "colored." I spent an hour with the dean and then gave a lecture to the entire school, including alumni. It was quite a moment to be back on campus. I was being introduced by a black dean to an audience of hundreds of Sam Zondis.

LESSON 7

═══════════

ADDRESS DIFFICULTIES
IN THE MOMENT

There are times in our lives where we fail to do the right thing. We know better, but we don't do better. It may be because we wish to avoid something difficult in the moment, but this is short-sighted. Avoidance doesn't make what is hard disappear. It makes it worse. Avoidance may in fact prolong a problem in a way that can never be rectified.

My relationship with Bob Pritzker ended in avoidance. He gave me a tremendous opportunity and was an understanding supporter of my career, yet I never properly thanked him. My last meeting with him was anticlimactic, and when I learned he had passed away, I regretted not having made more of an effort earlier. As time progressed, my relationship with Bob became more limited. Aspects of our personal and professional lives, which overlapped, became disjointed.

Bob was with his first wife, Audrey, when we first met. They were well established, and I was still a young professional making a career for myself. Audrey and Bob divorced in 1979, and she remains a friend to this day. During my years in Chicago, both at Northwestern and at IIT, Audrey was a great friend. She took my family into her family, and we spent time not only with her but with her children. The last time we saw Audrey and Bob together was at Audrey's seventieth birthday party. Bob attended, and to my knowledge they remained amicable. With Audrey it was always very personal, but with Bob it was a mixture of business and personal. Things were more complicated.

Bob was generous, and he had in many ways been helpful to me and our children. He arranged a summer job for our daughter, Ilana, at the Hyatt in New York. He arranged a job for our son, Lewis, in one of the Pritzker enterprises in Paris. He didn't have to, but he did. More importantly, he gave away millions of dollars to cultural institutions and causes.

He also had a defining quirk—he was extremely frugal. He was one of three sons of A. N. Pritzker, the founder of a Chicago business empire. He had plenty of money, but he did not waste a penny. It is simply who he was. I'm not speaking out of turn in mentioning this. He was famous for it. There was a joke—probably apocryphal but part of the Pritzker lore in Chicago—about him and his older brother having lunch together. The two of them would order a sandwich and split it in half.

On one occasion with his second wife, Irene, we were attending an antique fair in Chicago. Irene was taken with an Art Deco sculpture but anxious about buying it. Bob was uninterested in such things and thought it was a waste of money, but Irene convinced him it was okay for them to buy it. He agreed, under one condition. The sculpture had to be shipped from Chicago to New York and then mailed back to Chicago, to avoid sales tax.

One other time that we were with him was at the Ninety Fifth, a restaurant at the top of the John Hancock Center in Chicago and famous for its views. Getting to the restaurant was no easy feat. It required not one but two separate elevators. One evening, the four of us were having dinner together. Bob generously picked up the bill, and after dinner we went down the two elevators—ninety-four floors—to the street level. We crossed the street to the lot where we had parked. Bob suddenly realized in the parking lot that he had not had his parking ticket validated by the restaurant. Rather than pay the parking fee, he left us by the car, crossed the street, went up the two elevators to the ninety-fifth floor, validated the parking ticket, rode both elevators back down, walked back across the street, turned in his parking ticket, and then drove us home.

Again, while he saved relative pennies like this, he gave away tens of millions of dollars to universities, museums, and religious groups. He and his brother established the prestigious Pritzker Prize in Architecture, which is for architecture what the Nobel Prize is for medicine or economics. Its winners include Philip Johnson, I. M. Pei, and Frank Gehry. I always thought of his frugality as a funny quirk and his immense charitable generosity as the person he really was. In truth he was both: his frugality was generally focused toward himself, and his generosity was for others.

Here is where things get difficult. After moving to New York from Chicago, Barbara and I had fewer opportunities to see Bob and his third wife, Mari, though we would get together on occasion in Manhattan when they came to town. One of his daughters who lived on Long Island called us up and invited us to dinner with Bob at the hotel where he was staying. She said that he was very anxious to see us and that he had not been well of late.

When we arrived at the hotel dinner it was us, Bob and Mari, his daughter Karen, and her husband. It was an intimate scene, and I was distressed when I realized how ill Bob had become. I knew he had been suffering from Parkinson's and had difficulty with his speech and memory, but it was worse than I was prepared for. He asked me to sit next to him, and I helped cut his food. It was a difficult evening. I was of course pleased to see Bob after a couple of years but was shocked by the deterioration of his health. I wasn't sure I could handle it again.

About four months later, I received another call from Bob's daughter asking us to attend another dinner with Bob. She said, "Meyer, you know my Dad loves you." It was an overwhelming sentiment, and I just couldn't bear to see him in such a deteriorated condition. We made an excuse not to attend, and I regret this decision immensely. Bob had always behaved generously, and avoiding that encounter with him was selfish. I thought about how I felt at the moment and not about him. I have always felt shame that we did not attend that last dinner in New York with such a dear, close friend who had been so helpful to me and my family. It was not right. I knew it at the time, and today it still bothers me. We were not invited back, and I did not attempt to make a connection. Bob died a few months later. Don't make the same mistake I did. The pain of enduring an unwell friend will subside in time. If you do what I did, you will regret it always.

LESSON 8

BE GENEROUS

I have been fortunate in life to not have wants. I have lived well, and I have made the most of the opportunities I have been afforded. This is of course not true for everyone. Regardless, one must always act from a place of generosity. Generosity of time. Generosity of material resources. Generosity of opportunity. Generosity of spirit.

It's 1979, and I am in my office at Northwestern University. The phone rings, and Sol Kerzner is on the line from Johannesburg. He and I first met in Durban, South Africa, where he grew up. I was eight years old and he was eighteen. We met when I was on vacation with my parents over Passover. Sol's parents owned a small hotel, and we went there for a Passover Seder. Sol and I have been extremely close friends for many years, and it was common for us to call each other. I pick up the phone, and Sol says to me, "Meyer, I need a favor.

Sol Kerzner

Lucas Mangope, the chief of the Bophuthatswana tribe, has a son, Eddie, who wants to come to the Northwestern Kellogg Business School. Can you please take care of this for me?"

Lucas Mangope was the tribal chief—the equivalent of president or king—of a Bantustan, or territory, called Bophuthatswana. The tribe lived in an area designated by the white apartheid government about twenty-five miles from Johannesburg. Sol had proposed to the chief the building of a great resort in Mangope's territory, and the project was nearly completed. It was a massive development that included five-star hotels and the first major casino in South Africa. There was a stadium that housed world-title boxing matches and world-class entertainers including Frank Sinatra. Sun City, as it was called, was a Xanadu in the South African bush. We went to the opening and visited with Sol on numerous occasions. Sol's real estate dealings in Bophuthatswana were heavily dependent on his relationship with Mangope. Lucas Mangope held all the chips, and one of the chips he wished to cash with Sol was getting his son Eddie into Northwestern University.

After numerous discussions with the Office of Admissions, I was able to help get Eddie a place in the MBA program. I thought my responsibilities were done. Little did I know. Eddie arrived in Chicago in August and rang our doorbell. We had never met him. He introduced himself and then asked where he should put his bags. Barbara and I looked at each other and gulped. Eddie did not have a dorm room and had not thought to rent a room somewhere near campus. There was nothing to do but take him in, so we made Eddie a home on our third floor. Eddie seemed quite comfortable with his lodgings, which was great for him, but Barbara and I did not know what we were going to do with Eddie Mangope for an entire school year.

Two or three weeks after Eddie arrived, I received another call from Sol Kerzner. "Meyer, Eddie feels he needs a car. Can you please go out with him this weekend and help him buy a car?" What were we to do? Sol was a friend and Eddie was now our responsibility, so on Saturday, I took Eddie out to look for a car. We eventually found something suitable, and he was quite delighted with the freedom the car would give him. Sol had told me to call him if we were successful and he would send me a check to cover the purchase of the car.

That evening I called Sol in Johannesburg. He immediately asked: "Well, did Eddie get a car?"

I said, "Yes, we got him a red Ferrari." Silence, then, "*You . . . bought him . . . a . . . Ferrari!? Why did you do that?*"

"Well, Sol," I said, "we saw many cars, but he didn't like any of them, so I bought him what he wanted. Is this a problem?"

I held the phone and imagined Sol, a glass of whiskey in his hand and gulping it down as fast as he could. After about thirty seconds I said, "Sol, I'm just kidding. I didn't get him a Ferrari. I got him a second-hand Chevy." There was a huge sigh of relief in Johannesburg.

Eddie had been living in our house for some months when, one night, the phone rang at two AM. Barbara sleepily picked up the receiver and heard someone speaking in broken English on the other end asking to speak to Eddie Mangope. Dumbfounded as to why someone would call at this hour, Barbara asked with agitation, "Who are you and what do you want?"

"This call is from Rome. I am an emissary for His Holiness the pope." It was the Vatican. At this point, Barbara and I think we're going crazy. The man explains that the king of Bophuthatswana had had an audience with the pope a couple of days earlier and had mentioned that his unfortunate son was in the United States at a college in Chicago without a place to live. The aides around the pope heard this and naturally called the archbishop of Chicago. They explained that the pope would like the archbishop of Chicago to find a suitable apartment for the king of Bophuthatswana's son, who was currently living in an attic in Evanston. The caller, apparently unconcerned about the time difference, wanted to tell Eddie that the Vatican had found a suitable apartment for him.

So I went up three sets of stairs to fetch Eddie to the kitchen, where he could speak to the Vatican about his new apartment. Two days later, Barbara, Eddie, and I packed up his things and loaded his car. Barbara and I watched him drive off. She turned to me and said, "Does this mean I'm not going to have to wash his underwear anymore?" It did. But I could not have imagined us doing it any other way, friends helping friends in need.

LESSON 9

PLACE MATTERS

During my life and career I have had the opportunity to travel throughout the world and live in some extraordinary places. In all of the places I've lived, I've learned the simple truth that place matters. Wherever you live, make the most of it, and throw yourself headlong into your community. This became clear to me when I moved back to New York as dean of Columbia Business School.

In 1989 I was invited by Columbia Business School's search committee to visit the campus in May. The first person I interviewed with was Lionel Pincus. At that time he was a member of the Board of Trustees of Columbia University. He and Jerry Speyer would go on to be elected co-chairs of the board in the early 1990s. Like me, both came to Columbia University via Columbia Business School.

Lionel Pincus

Lionel was chairman of the New York–based private equity firm Warburg Pincus. He was a well-known and important figure in the culture of the city. The interview was somewhat conventional until I asked him, "Lionel, what kind of endowment does Columbia University have, and, in particular, what kind of endowment does Columbia Business School have?" I meant this fairly straightforwardly in terms of dollars and cents. His response was not what I expected.

He said, "I'm not sure where to start. The primary endowment is New York City—it is Lincoln Center and Carnegie
Hall. It is the Metropolitan Museum and the Museum of
Modern Art. It is Broadway. It is the Yankees. It is the New
York Giants. It is the Empire State Building and Central
Park West. It is banking and media. It is the most important
global city in the world. That's its primary endowment." He
then continued with the kind of answer I had expected initially. "In addition, the university has a financial endowment
of approximately two billion dollars. The business school's
endowment is minute. It is less than twenty million dollars.
In fact, that is going to be one of the first problems that the
new dean is going to have to deal with. The financial endowment of the business school is not competitive."

But Lionel underlined that students who come to Columbia are coming to Columbia University in the city of New
York. What they are getting is something that students cannot get elsewhere. They are getting a university, a unique
city, and a global education. He said that at Columbia "we
expect our students to be engaged in the city, we expect our
faculty to be involved and engaged in the city, and we know
that our alumni play leadership roles in the city. If you become
dean of Columbia Business School, you will need to become
part of the life of that city. You will need to go to Lincoln
Center and the Metropolitan Museum. You will need to
walk through Central Park. You will need to join organizations and committees and the boards that are important to
Columbia and therefore to the city. I know you have come

from New Orleans via Chicago. Both are wonderful cities with their own atmosphere and assets, but nothing like the scale of New York."

I remembered Lionel's observations and advice and took them to heart. When I was appointed dean and gave my first welcome address to an incoming MBA class, I stood in front of them and said, "Welcome to Columbia University in the city of New York. Welcome to Columbia Business School. I want to be sure that everybody knows where they are. This is New York City. It is not Hanover, New Hampshire; it is not Ann Arbor, Michigan; and it is not New Orleans, Louisiana. It is New York City, the greatest global city in the world. If you don't understand that, and if you cannot cope with that, then you are in the wrong place. Crossing the street at Broadway and 116th Street is a big deal not to be taken lightly." Place matters.

I continued, "People at our school, Columbia, need to be engaged. They should not stand idly on the sidewalk. They need to get into the traffic. They should take advantage of what the entire university and the city of New York have to offer. You can't graduate from Columbia without ever having left the campus. You need to leave it with memories of the school, your fellow students, and the faculty, but also of the restaurants, museums, Broadway shows, and Lincoln Center. If you are successful at Columbia and in New York, you could be, should be, and will be successful anywhere in the world. Columbia will globalize your view of the world. I know this because I was a student here."

Getting involved with the New Yorkness of New York has served me well. During my fifteen years as dean, I was appointed to numerous boards of directors of businesses with connections to the city. I served for twenty-four years on the board of Macy's. I served on Primedia, a KKR-controlled company. I was a long-serving member on the board of Revlon. I was invited to join the board of the New York City Ballet, on which I have served for two terms.

Barbara and I became very involved with Lincoln Center. We attended the ballet, the opera, and the Philharmonic once or twice a month. We were in and out of the Met, the Frick, and MoMA, to name but a few of the world's great museums.

Opening Bell for Macy's, Inc., at NYSE

Barbara Feldberg

When you're engaged in the life of New York's elite, you end up attending black-tie events and dinners with some regularity. It is a truly thrilling experience to live and participate in the life of New York City. Having said that, we do take time off. We have a home in Vail, Colorado, and go skiing twice a year and visit for a couple of weeks in the summer. We are always happy for the break, but we are always delighted to be back in Manhattan, in our apartment on Central Park West, across from Central Park. New York City is a place for young people with energy and old people with energy. We are all energized by the city.

LESSON 10

ENGAGE WITH ALL OF YOUR CONSTITUENCIES BUT KNOW WHO COMES FIRST

My position as dean gave me access to all that New York had to offer, including all the big shots in politics and business. We had regular events—and still do—at our home that included guests like Mike Bloomberg, Larry Summers, Bibi Netanyahu, Ross Perot, and Dick Cheney, to name but a few of the movers and shakers who have sat at our dining-room table with faculty, students, and alumni. It is easy in this position to get carried away with the names in bold, but the dean of a school is responsible to the full range of students, staff, faculty, administrators, and benefactors. A well-run organization provides for the needs of its entire constituency, not just the celebrities. It's not enough just to manage up. A good leader engages with all of his or her constituencies, and at a university there is no group that matters more than the students.

I recall Columbia University's 1998 commencement, when I was in the second five-year term of my deanship. I'm sitting in my office behind my desk. My door is open, and I hear a knock. I look up and see an elegant middle-aged woman standing at the door. I immediately begin to rise. She says, "Please don't get up, Professor Feldberg. My name is Mrs. Rockefeller, and I want you to know, that I know, that if not for you, my son would not have graduated from business school today." I begin to get up, but she turns and walks out of the dean's suite straight into the lobby. There is no better feeling one can have as an educator than knowing that you have helped someone accomplish their goals.

I exit Uris onto the Columbia campus, which is dotted with hundreds of faculty in their glorious academic regalia. There are red, blue, black, and scarlet gowns with black velvet hats and hoods of different colors, denoting various academic careers and degrees. There are thousands of students in blue gowns together with their families. They are wandering around the campus after the commencement ends. It is a very special day.

I, too, was once one of those graduating students and recall the pride that these students feel in their accomplishments. In my mind I am transported back to commencement in May 1965, where I took Barbara by the hand and walked her across the campus to the Azaleas, outside the rotunda of Low Library. It was the place and moment that I asked her to marry me. She said yes, and we told my parents

Leon and Sarah Feldberg at college graduation

and her mother before going into Uris Hall for the Business School reception. I know how happy that mother and her graduating son felt that day. It is a once-in-a-lifetime moment.

Columbia, like all great universities, has many constituencies. There are students but also faculty, administrators, alumni, recruiters, board members, donors, and competitors, all with different and at times competing needs. But for a dean or university president, there are a set of unique, unbreakable links in the chain. First come the applicants, followed by those who are admitted and become the students. At the end of their studies students become graduates, and after graduation they are alumni. The alumni—we hope

(top) King Abdullah
(bottom) Henry Kissinger

and expect—will become successful leaders in their chosen fields. They are linked to the recruiters who have hired them after graduation, who in turn are networked to the donors who help support the institution. Alumni marry and have children, and the cycle continues.

As a dean I realized that the university with its many constituencies requires its leaders to be available all the time, to multiple constituencies who may or may not feel comfortable with one another. At the school level it is the dean's responsibility to make sure that the quality of the students is maintained and enhanced, that the teaching skills of the faculty are excellent, that the curriculum is appropriate and forward looking, that the research enhances the image of the institution as well as the image of the professors, and that the administrators are making sure that all the machinery associated with a great institution functions smoothly. The dean must interact with alumni from all walks of life, from those just starting out in their careers to those internationally renowned for their accomplishments.

Because a business school is a professional school, the dean of the Columbia Business School must be in continual contact with corporate recruiters from the kinds of industries that appeal to the Ivy League student, from investment banking and consulting to nonprofits, whether based in New York or on the other side of the globe in China. Students go to business school to get jobs, and these are the recruiters who will ultimately hire them, giving them the opportunity to grow into leaders in their fields. Every constituent member of the university is entitled to and expects to be "taken care of." For a dean, this is a seventy- to eighty-hour week. Every constituency feels it is important, and every constituency is in fact important—each must be taken care of if an institution is to thrive—but it is the success of the students and the quality of their education that are our top priorities.

LESSON 11

LEAD FROM THE FRONT

In a position of leadership it's easy to cordon yourself off, hurling missives and directives from a remote office suite. An organization's staff relies on its leader for direction. This comes across not just in what the leader does but how he does it. Good leaders lead from the front and set an example for the norms of behavior within the organization. When I arrived as dean of Columbia Business School in 1989, the institution was in desperate need of new leadership—of people willing to get into the trenches.

In 1989, the business school had just been ranked fifteenth in the nation. This may seem fine, but at a university routinely ranked in the top ten in the world, this doesn't cut it. Every constituency was angry, particularly the students. The ranking had compromised their employment opportunities. The faculty was embarrassed and had low self-esteem. The alumni had been walking away from supporting the business school. The physical plant was in a state of great disrepair, and the administrators were being blamed. The curriculum in 1989 had been allowed to stagnate. Some of the faculty was still using material that I had studied in 1963. Columbia Business School in 1989 was an unhappy institution.

Something visible and meaningful had to be done. I had to find a way to recapture the institution's self-esteem. I had to make myself visible and available. Steps both small and giant were necessary. A small step was that I never changed any of the furniture in the dean's suite. My desk actually had a brick underneath one of its legs, and it remained that way for fifteen years.

At the other extreme, we assembled a group of the most senior and most admired faculty members to review and renew the curriculum. We started allowing the students to score faculty performance in the classroom, and we published the results. We reconnected with alumni to get their buy-in to the new strategy we were developing.

In my first couple of months as dean, I visited some of our most prominent alumni, including Henry Kravis, cofounder of KKR; Jerry Chazen, cofounder of Liz Claiborne; Russ Carson, cofounder of WCAS; Ben Rosen, chairman of Compaq Computers; and Lord Sainsbury, chairman of Sainsbury, to name just a few. I put together a board of overseers that included forty-five members from around the world. This captured the imagination of the recruiters, faculty, students, and thousands of other alumni.

To get closer to the constituencies who are part of the community on a day-to-day basis, I created a dean's "Fix-It" committee. For six months I moved my desk into the middle of the lobby of Uris Hall. I would sit at my desk with different administrators and encourage students and faculty to bring me their complaints and problems. Over these six months, hundreds of people came to talk to me, and dozens of changes were made based on what they had to say. I would try to respond to their complaints and questions then and there. In some cases, I would tell the student or students that they could fix the problem and that I would allocate a budget amount for them to do so. In other cases, I would explain that nothing could be done to fix the matter but that we would try to find a way around it.

We put sheets of paper along the walls highlighting the issues we were addressing, who was responsible, and what sort of funds would be allocated to fix it. The dean's "Fix-It" committee brought me very close to the students, administrators, and faculty, all of whom are part of the life of the school on a daily basis. At the end of the six months I moved back into my office full time, but I always kept my door open and always went to visit faculty and administrators in their offices rather than having them come to mine.

For almost my entire deanship I would try to go into what was then known as the Uris Deli, in other words the school cafeteria, at around seven-forty-five AM. I'd buy a cup of coffee and sit at a table in the middle of the room reading the *Wall Street Journal*. Whenever I did this, people came up to chat with me—students, administrators, and faculty. Over time, the conversations became increasingly observably enthusiastic, and the attitude and demeanor of all of the school's constituencies improved.

Two years later, when the next *Business Week* school ranking survey came out, Columbia Business School had climbed to number 8. Three years after that, *US News and World Report* ranked Columbia number 3. Applications went up. Student selectivity went up. GMAT test scores went up. Selectivity went from 40 percent into the low teens. More recruiters visited campus, and more offers were made. Leadership starts from the top.

Business Week article

LESSON 12

WIELD POWER RESPONSIBLY

There are times when we have power over others and we use it appropriately, but there is also the temptation to use that power selfishly. The line between the use and the abuse of power is easiest to see at a distance. And sometimes we lose sight of it when friends and family are concerned. An episode in which I abused my power that I am ashamed of concerns my son when he was a student at Columbia Business School and how I treated an instructor in one of his classes.

My son, Lewis, graduated from the University of Chicago and was admitted to Columbia Business School in the early 1990s. He was a very good to excellent student. One of his instructors was a man I had had several unfortunate incidents with early on in my deanship. He was arrogant, but then so was I. A group of faculty and I were attending a conference in Cleveland. At the end of the first day, we were getting into the elevator, and the then chairman of the company hosting the conference greeted me and said he was "extremely impressed with my leadership of Columbia Business School." The elevator was filled with executives and some of my colleagues. This professor heard the comment, turned around, and said to the chairman, "Actually, his leadership has not been very good." There was dead silence until the elevator emptied out on the ground floor. This professor had needlessly picked a fight with the wrong guy. He then went one step further and harassed my son, who was in his class.

From that point on, he didn't exist as far as I was concerned. I made his life difficult. Other faculty members began to distance themselves from him.

A couple of years before I stepped down as dean, he called me and asked if he could come and see me. It was the first time we had spoken in a number of years. I agreed to meet with him. That same day he walked down to my office. We sat opposite each other at my conference table. He put his hands on the table, looked at me, and said, "You have placed a death sentence on me." I looked at him unsympathetically. He then said, "I know I made two blunders, and I want to apologize for one of them." I said nothing. "I want to apologize for using my professorial power to harass your son." I said nothing. We sat and looked at each other for a couple of minutes, after which he stood up and walked out. We never spoke again.

Twenty years later, I know that I was harsh. He was a jerk and a spiteful one at that, but I had abused my power in a way that reflected poorly on me. Why should I have cared if

In the classroom

he dismissed my leadership in front of me to a corporate executive? That reflects poorly on him. His mistreatment of my son as his student also reflected poorly on him. Lewis was an adult and could handle himself. When you are in a position of power, take the high road. If subordinates are on the wrong track, let them know. Be constructive, and you will achieve a better end.

LESSON 13

MAKE AN EXTRA EFFORT
FOR TOP TALENT

When I became dean at Columbia Business School, I knew that the faculty were waiting and watching to see what I would do to enhance their effectiveness and their capacity to recruit additional talent. As anyone who has worked in a university knows, when push comes to shove, the faculty has enormous positive and negative power over the dean and the school. The more illustrious the faculty is, the more highly is the institution viewed. The faculty must be seen by their peers to be outstanding. The dean and the university need to place great value on the reputation of the faculty. The dean has to find a way to increase revenue to support faculty recruitment. Special perks need to be given to key faculty members, who will be the jewels in the crown that is the reputation of the institution. I made it my mission to get one of those stars. In raising an organization's reputation one must make an extra effort for top talent.

In 2000, Joe Stiglitz, who had been chairman of the Council of Economic Advisors and a chief economist at the World Bank, left Washington and went back to Stanford University. He and his wife Anya wanted to return to the East Coast. Joe was a very important and eminent scholar and a public intellectual, a professor who would draw students, faculty, and benefactors and immediately raise the reputation of the school. When he came on the market, several top-tier universities other than Columbia also wanted him. That's tough competition.

I needed some support from Henry Kravis, one of our most prominent board members. I called and asked if I could bring Joe to have lunch with him. Of course he agreed. A week later, Joe was in New York, and we went to have lunch with Henry. It was a most agreeable lunch. Kravis did an excellent job of placing the business school within the university and the university within the city. After lunch I went back to my office, and Joe went back to his hotel.

On the ride back to my office, Henry telephoned me.

"Meyer, was the lunch OK?"

"Yes," I said.

"Why was it so important for me to see this guy?"

"Because, Henry," I said, "he's going to win a Nobel Prize."

"What do you mean, he's going to win a Nobel Prize?"

Joseph Stiglitz

"Henry, I'm telling you, Stiglitz is going to win a Nobel Prize." Henry laughed at the end of the conversation, appreciating my confidence.

In the end Joe Stiglitz accepted Columbia's offer, and he joined the university and business school. Six months later I was proven right. He won a Nobel Prize. Henry remembered to call me after the announcement.

Intellectual talent is vital to the success of an academic institution. The research status of the faculty among other institutions is critical. On a percentage basis I probably put more money behind faculty recruiting than any other line item in the school's budget. Having world-renowned scholars walking the halls, classrooms, and campus of the university and the business school is an imperative.

After stepping down as dean, I remained a professor at the university on a leave of absence. I must say that Lee Bollinger, the president of the university, has greatly enhanced the stature of Columbia University. In 2018, the *Wall Street Journal* ranked Columbia University the number 2 university in the nation. As I look back on my fifty-three-year relationship at Columbia—keep in mind I was a student there in 1963—I recognize that success requires outstanding execution but that without a vision and a strategy, the execution itself is not sufficient. Top talent combines leadership and execution.

LESSON 14

═══════════

BE MENTORED
AND BE A MENTOR

Over many years, you come to realize and understand that there are people in your life that have advised you, helped you, guided you, and mentored you. You also realize that there are people in your life that you have mentored and that come to have valued your advice and guidance. Nobody does it alone. We learn from others both how to do things and how not to do things, and it is incumbent upon us to pass that experience along to others.

Mentoring or being mentored is something that we frequently do not understand at the time. Years later, as we look back on our lives and careers, we are able to identify the people who we've mentored and the people who have mentored us. During my early years in Chicago, I was blessed with having a relationship with Don Jacobs, who built the Kellogg School of Management at Northwestern University into one of the top five schools in the nation. Don Jacobs was known as the "Dean of Deans" in the business school world. He and I saw each other almost every day during my three years at Northwestern. We would end the day by sitting in the sauna, talking about life.

I tried to emulate Don in many ways. He was always visible with the students and with the faculty. He amplified the reputation of the school by visiting major universities around the world. He created executive education programs that attracted leaders from around the world to Kellogg. As I look back on my days as a dean, I recognize that many of my successful decisions stem from working with and watching Don Jacobs.

Mentoring and guiding need not necessarily be a one-on-one process. Exposure to the ideas of others can set us on a course that forever after shapes the way we see the world. One of the giants in my life in this respect was Milton Friedman. He was awarded the Nobel Prize in Economics in 1976. He was a global figure, and everywhere he went he was lionized.

My position in academia meant that I had the ability to expand my relationship with his work on the page to real life. In 1976 I invited Milton and his wife, Rose, to visit us in South Africa, and they spent nearly three weeks with us. We drove and flew them around the country, and everywhere we went he spoke to standing-room-only crowds. I arranged a lunch for him with the president of South Africa. Harry Oppenheimer, the chairman of DeBeers and Anglo American

Milton Friedman

at the time, arranged for us to visit and go down the deepest shaft mine in the world. As I recall, it was 12,000 feet underground.

We also enjoyed a world-class dinner at the Oppenheimers' in honor of Milton. Over an extremely elaborate meal, Milton explained to the twenty guests his philosophy of economics. He was providing guidance and mentoring to a group of twenty exceptionally sophisticated leaders. At

Zulu Land: Rose Friedman, Gatsha Buthelezi, Barbara Feldberg

every major event in each city he spoke to hundreds of people who wanted to know what he recommended for South Africa and for the world. He was mentoring hundreds of people simultaneously. Whether it was in a classroom, a small study group, or a convention hall, people wanted to know what Milton Friedman had to say about economics and its impact on a nation-state, a village, or a single individual.

Being a mentor to others is as rewarding, if not more rewarding, than being mentored. A couple of weeks after I moved into the dean's office at Columbia, I identified a young assistant professor who had outstanding teaching skills, was highly regarded by the student body, and who understood how to create a curriculum. Safwan Masri was in his late twenties when I walked up to his office on the fourth floor. His door was open, so I walked right in. Much later he told me that he got a shock because he thought the dean was coming in to berate him about something or other. He popped out of his seat, and I told him to sit back down. I sat down in front of him at his desk. "Safwan," I said, "I want you downstairs in the dean's suite. I'm appointing you vice dean for student affairs and curriculum." It's true what they say: sometimes people's jaws do drop.

Safwan Masri

A week later, Safwan was ensconced in his office imme-diately next to mine. A large number of faculty members had not met him and did not even know who he was. Those who did know couldn't understand how an untenured, twenty-eight-year-old assistant professor could be appointed a vice dean.

Safwan served as vice dean for my entire fifteen years, during which time we became close friends—he and I, and he and the rest of my family. Safwan is one of the most engaging people Barbara and I know. The students always trust him to look after them. He deserved an opportunity. I feel fortunate that I was in a position to be able to make it possible. We learned from each other as colleagues.

Over the fifteen years of our professional relationship I came to understand that I was mentoring Safwan for leader-ship. He had the personality and the talent to be a leader, but at the same time he needed to learn what he didn't know and what he shouldn't do, what he had to do and how to deal with thousands of students and a faculty of a hundred PhDs. What he needed was mentoring. It's something that we all need because we can't possibly know what we don't know. Mentors are guides who can help a mentee learn how to navigate the kinds of successes and failures that happen within organizations time and again.

Safwan is still at Columbia, but now he reports directly to the president of the university. His title is professor and exec-utive vice president for global centers and global develop-ment at Columbia University. His story is the quintessential one of moving on and moving up. He travels the world for Columbia. He calls from Rio, then from Amman on his way to Shanghai. Then he's back in New York for two weeks and it's off to Nigeria and Tel Aviv. Safwan is an unusual mix. He is agreeable and endearing but at the same time determined, competitive, and energetic. I take vicarious enjoyment in watching him grow in his life and career, an upside benefit of being a mentor!

LESSON 15

TEND TO YOUR FRIENDSHIPS

L ooking back over a life and career, I've come to understand that relationships and friendships don't always last. There will be people with whom you may develop deep and meaningful relationships that turn out to be circumstantial. At the worst, there are people whose friendship is based purely out of self-interest. They believe that you can be helpful to them. They believe that the organization you are leading can be helpful to them. They believe it is good to be seen with you. You, too, may believe that they can be helpful to you. There also are friendships that exist because what brings you together is a shared goal or objective. This often occurs in the workplace, and when circumstances change and that shared project is no longer there, the friendship disappears. Good friends can be hard to find, and friendships, like marriage, require active cultivation by both sides. It's not always evident in the moment who is a true friend and who is not. Treat people well and know that sometimes relationships end.

During my fifteen years at Columbia Business School, I became friendly with a New York–based banker. We interacted a lot and traveled in many of the same professional and social circles. I made special efforts—deservedly so—to get him involved with and gain recognition from the school. We had a warm friendship, but, I realize in retrospect, it was more of a transactional relationship than a true friendship. I heard from him regularly when he needed advice for colleagues or acquaintances about Columbia Business School. I think I was always appropriately helpful.

Our relationship was based on my position rather than something deeper. This became clear the year I retired. Efforts I made to continue the relationship failed to generate a response. I called, left messages, dropped notes to no avail. I guess it turned out that there was nothing more I could do for him. What did he need me for? There was a new dean who could take care of him.

I realized that this person was not unique and that there were others like him. These were important people with whom I had important, meaningful, but in the end transactional relationships. They were based not on us as two friends but as two people occupying institutional positions. Our relationship was about the institutions that we worked for and the position that we occupied. I hadn't prepared myself for this, but this was naïveté on my part. Circumstantial friendships place in sharp relief the importance of friendships that

Best friends: Russ Carson, Barbara Feldberg, Meyer Feldberg, Judy Carson

may start out at work but become something deeper. There were some truly wonderful friends whom I continue to see regularly that I came to know through Columbia University. These relationships turned out to be personal as well as professional. Russ Carson is the epitome of such a friend.

LESSON 16

ACTIVELY PARTICIPATE
IN YOUR COMMUNITY

I t was a long, very long, tedious day. Barbara is standing behind me on the escalator at Newark Airport. I look down at her and say, "I just can't do this anymore." Three days after coming back from Colorado I was scheduled to fly from New York to Johannesburg for a board meeting. I was the deputy chairman of Sappi, one of the two or three largest paper companies in the world. Sappi's head office was in Johannesburg, and the company had six board meetings a year, three of which were in South Africa. It was my ninth year on the board, and I had simply run out of gas. It was too much long-haul travel. I went to two more board meetings and retired.

Over a period of nearly twenty years, I served on a number of corporate boards, a few cultural boards, and six community and educational boards. My board experience was extremely demanding but exceptionally valuable. I learned a lot serving on Macy's board for twenty-four years. I served as president of NYC Global Partners, a board established by Mayor Michael Bloomberg and designed to manage New York's relationships with other global cities. There I learned even more. The greatest asset of being on a board of substance is that you're able to give and that you're able to get. I learned a great deal from these boards.

I also believe that I had much to offer the institutions on whose boards I served. All the boards were interesting, and I was often able to transfer my knowledge from one board to another. I also found myself bumping into the same leaders in the community on many of the boards. It is a mistake to think that boards are like clubs. They are not. They are extremely demanding of the time, the knowledge, the information, and the judgment that board members bring to the institution.

As we all know, it doesn't always work. There are great boards and rotten boards. Boards with integrity and boards with greedy people who use the board for their own advantage. Great boards can become rotten boards. The leadership of the board and the members of the boards must be vigilant at all times. It is not only about finance, marketing, manufacturing, or technology, ballet music or education; it is about the people to whom and for whom you are responsible. The employees, the students, the dancers, the scientists— they all have a right to expect the board to do their duty with integrity. I would like to say that I never served on a board that didn't sweep things under the rug, but that would not be true. I am pleased to say I opposed hiding what should be visible and never gave a bye to people who should not be part of the enterprise.

Across all organizations and institutions on which I served over the past thirty years, I probably attended close to a thousand board meetings. The arithmetic is simple: 5 meetings a year × 7 boards × 30 years = 1,000 board meetings. I must have been *mad*. I'm still mad. I have, however, become more sensible. I have dropped boards that have become less meaningful to me or to the city, country, industry, university, business, or community they serve. Many board meetings are all-day or multiday affairs with no break, and participants must always be "on." They involve breakfast. They involve lunch. They involve receptions. They involve dinners. They involve contributions to events that the institution supports or that members of the board would like other members to support.

Imagine you are on a corporate board. Your meeting begins with breakfast at 8:30 AM. The meeting runs through lunch. There is a reception at the end of the first day to which spouses and employees are invited. The reception ends. The visitors can leave, but the board then has a dinner. The next morning there is another breakfast followed by a board meeting that ends at noon. Lunch is optional. That night you have been invited to attend a gala for a very worthy institution that is supported by either the board or by individuals on the board. You go home. You shower. You put on an evening suit, and you and your spouse go to a 5:30 PM reception at a hotel, a museum, or a university for cocktails, followed by dinner, during which there are three speeches, one thanking the gala committee and the donors, one introducing the honoree, and then the honoree him- or herself. It's now 10 PM. The evening is over and everyone rushes for the doors. These events are a little like traveling. At some point in time, you say to your spouse or she says to you, "you know what, I'm done." But with a little time and reflection you're right back at it again.

NYC Global Partners was one of the most interesting and pleasant boards on which I served. The board was an enhancement of what had previously been the Sister City program. Michael Bloomberg and his colleagues and in particular his sister, Marjorie Tiven, created NYC Global Partners. The organization hosted events in the city and around the world. An enormous amount of attention was given to climate change and school education. The organization arranged visits for mayors from around the world. Nearly one hundred global cities were partners in the organization, and dozens of mayors visited New York for programs sponsored by NYC Global Partners. One of the final events that I attended as president of NYC Global Partners was a reception to honor New York as host city to the diplomatic and consular community and NYC Global Partners for connecting New York to cities around the world. The event took place at the United Nations. Many city agencies attended, and I was honored to follow Michael Bloomberg and Marjorie Tiven in making remarks on all that NYC Global Partners

Mike Bloomberg, Meyer Feldberg, Russ Carson

had accomplished. NYC Global Partners made meaningful connections and forged partnerships on a variety of important social issues. It was an ideal mix of entrepreneurial innovation and civic mindedness.

Not all board meetings and board events are so agreeable. It is important, as a board member, always to remember you are there to serve the interests of the organization or institution and its consumers or patrons, not yourself, your fellow board members, or the organizational hierarchy. I have a vivid memory of being threatened at a board meeting by the chairman of the board in front of all the other board members and a number of managers.

The chairman of this board was the controlling share-holder of the company. He proposed to the board that we approve a resolution allowing him to exercise a transaction that the independent directors of the board believed should be reviewed by a special committee of the board who would be charged with hiring a financial institution and a legal firm to advise them on the appropriateness of the proposal. Unfortunately, I was elected chairman of this special com-mittee. After numerous meetings with and studies by the outside lawyers and the financial institution, my colleagues on the committee and I were advised to recommend to the full board that the resolution not be approved. This process took place over a period of several months.

When the work of the special committee was complete, a board meeting was called, and I announced to the full board, including the chairman, that the special committee could not recommend to the board that it approve the pro-posal. The chairman became enraged. He jumped up from his seat and literally ran around the table screaming at me in particular but at the other members of the board as well. In a fifty-year career I had never heard language like that, and I had never been attacked and abused so violently. The board meeting ended, and we filed out of the room.

That evening I had an overseas flight to attend the meet-ing of another organization. On my way to the airport, I called the in-house counsel and informed him that I would be resigning from the board in a couple of days, after my return. He pleaded with me not to resign. He agreed that the chairman's behavior had been inappropriate but that if I resigned it would be an embarrassment to the chairman, the board, and to the company. I told him I was sorry about that, but my mind was made up. He asked if I would be prepared to speak to the chairman before going public. I agreed. He said the chairman would call me.

A couple of minutes later, the chairman called me in the car. He was exceptionally apologetic. He did not know what came over him. He asked me to tell him what he needed to do in order for me not to resign. I was quiet for a moment, and then I said, "I might reconsider if you call every other member of the board individually and apologize for the way you treated me and the rest of the board." He was quiet for a moment and said he would do so. I said I would wait to see what happened over the course of the few days while I was away. Before hanging up, the chairman said to me, "Meyer, you know I love you." I am not making this up. "Meyer, you know I love you." He had an odd way of showing it.

I remained on the board for another five years. I did the job I was there to perform and then I stepped down.

Institutions that are established to work for nonprofit organizations frequently attract the most generous and thoughtful individuals. University boards, community boards, climate boards, cultural boards, and religious boards all have a vision of how they can make our lives better, and in many ways they do. It is not about scale but intensity. Not-for-profit boards generally include members who are committed to the philosophy of the institution and the rightness of the purpose of the institution. Such boards inevitably depend upon the commitment and generosity of board members and donors. Fundraising ends up being a critically important function or activity for the institution and for the board members. It only works if you really believe in the vision and mission of the institution.

I have served on over a dozen not-for-profit boards, including one institution that was established decades ago and became the best of its kind in the world. I refer to the New York City Ballet. What I observed at the NYC Ballet was the institution's intense commitment to talent. Ballet dancers can be good, they can be very good, and then they can be New York City Ballet good—the best in the world. The two creators of this phenomenal enterprise were George Balanchine and Jerome Robbins. Their work and their choreography have traveled the world. When Balanchine retired, his protégé Peter Martins became the ballet master–in-chief. Peter was able to maintain the extraordinary reputation of the New York City Ballet for thirty years. On the many occasions that Peter and I spoke, I always reminded him that he had a unique eye for talent. He could look at a seven-year-old and tell whether the child had the capacity to be a dancer. During my years on the board, I rarely saw an error in his judgment. The New York City Ballet has become a well-endowed institution with extremely generous donors who are committed balletomanes. People don't go to a ballet performance; they go to multiple ballet performances.

My wife and I probably attend the ballet ten to twelve times a year.

A second board I am intensely committed to is the Columbia Business School Board of Overseers. This was a board that I created from scratch in 1989. During the fifteen years that I was dean, I grew the board to forty-five people. Almost all the board members are Columbia graduates, some going back as far as the 1940s. All of them had an intense loyalty to Columbia University and to the Columbia Business School. The board was prepared and anxious to enhance the standing and status of Columbia Business School. They understood that creating a significant endowment, adding new academic centers, providing merit scholarships, and recruiting great faculty—including Nobel Prize winners—was what would make Columbia Business School a great global institution.

I built the board of overseers slowly. I visited with senior alumni in Europe, Asia, and South America. Of forty-five board members, twenty were not from the United States. The first chairman of the board was Ben Rosen, who had recruited me for the deanship of Columbia Business School in the first place. I recruited Jerome "Jerry" Chazen, chairman and one of the four founding partners of Liz Claiborne, to the board. He asked what my most important initial strategy would be for Columbia Business School. I said, "Jerry, I want to internationalize the school. I want to globalize the curriculum, the faculty, the case studies, the materials. I want our students to come from around the world and to be taught by faculty from multiple geographies." Jerry was enthusiastic. Through his own business he had personally traveled the world looking for designers and manufacturers. He told me that many of his competitors felt ill at ease once they left the Anglo-Saxon world. For him it was an adventure.

After we discussed the need for and the strategy for globalization, he asked me what I wanted from him. I said it would be an expensive business and that I was hoping he would commit a couple of million dollars to build the program. He looked at me and said, "That's no good." I was disappointed. He said, "You can do nothing with two million dollars; what you need is ten million dollars." It was the first time I had been driven *up* by a donor. Ten million dollars! It would be the biggest gift the school had ever received and certainly the largest gift that I had ever attracted. I left his office floating on a cloud.

The next day I called a faculty meeting to announce the creation of the Chazen Institute, with a ten-million-dollar gift from Jerry Chazen. Thirty-three years later, the Chazen Institute remains one of the most important institutes of Columbia Business School. It attracts faculty from around the world. It sends students to different countries on assignment. It provides money for research and academic materials. For me in my first year it was a home run. Fortunately, many subsequent home runs occurred. Board members such as Henry Kravis, Lord Sainsbury, Art Samburg, and Ben Rosen all began to invest heavily in Columbia Business School. Russ Carson was the first board member to push for a new building. We opened the new tiered classroom and E-MBA building across the street. During my fifteen years as dean, the board members became a family through our shared commitment to a common cause.

I have served on numerous corporate boards that were successful and helped me grow my knowledge and skills in business, and I've served on many boards that have helped me enhance the intellectual and performing arts of our city. It is particularly gratifying to know that at almost every board meeting I will be meeting people from other boards on which I served. It is one of the great blessings of living in the greatest global city in the world. Lionel Pincus was right when he told me in 1989, as I was being recruited to Columbia, that the Columbia endowment is New York City. It is the Metropolitan Museum. It is the New York City Ballet. It is Columbia University. It is Broadway. The Yankees. The Giants. The Philharmonic. The Empire State Building. The Statue of Liberty.

LESSON 17

STAY ACTIVE

There are people who eagerly count down the days to their retirement with the goal of spending their so-called golden years—if they can afford it—as leisurely as they can. I am no such person. F. Scott Fitzgerald wrote that there are no second acts in American life. While it was not my aim to prove this wrong, my postretirement career as dean has proven as long lasting as my time in academic administration. If you, like me, find the concept of retirement inconceivable, fear not, for second acts are indeed possible.

My last day in the office as dean of Columbia Business School was June 30, 2004. I had announced my intention to step down in June 2003, in order to ensure that the school and the university had sufficient time to search for a new dean. Before stepping down, President Lee Bollinger and the trustees of Columbia University very generously appointed me dean emeritus and maintained my professorial position as a faculty member on leave.

During my final year I received many offers and opportunities from banks, corporations, not-for-profit organizations, and private equity firms to join their organization in either a leadership position or as a colleague. In November 2004, I accepted an offer from Morgan Stanley as a senior advisor to the bank. It was one of three institutions that early on invited me to join their firms. During that same period, I was recruited by the Hoover Institute as its director and the World Trade Center Memorial Foundation to serve as its president and chief executive officer. They all offered more or less the same position and opportunity and were seeking an individual with deep reach into the corporate community around the country and the world. As dean of a global business school, I am part of a large network of leaders of major private-sector institutions. After much thought, I accepted the offer from Morgan Stanley, which allowed me to stay in New York and was an opportunity to move out of the academic and nonprofit world in a non-board-member capacity. I joined the bank almost immediately after my stepping down as dean, and I am deep into my second decade as a full-time senior advisor.

I am healthy and fit, but I am obviously not a young man. I am clearly of retirement age, and people ask me all the time why I have not retired. Why do I get up in the morning, have a yogurt, and then walk two and a half miles to the Morgan Stanley office in Midtown from my apartment uptown off of Central Park? I do it because it is part of how intensely engaged Barbara and I are in our life in New York City. In any given week, we may attend a performance at the New York City Ballet, an Opera at the Met, or a reception at the opening of a gallery. Barbara has not retired, either. She has her own professional life as an artist, and she paints daily in her studio. It's simple: these are the activities that keep us

Barbara Feldberg at NYCB opening night

growing and developing in spite of the fact that we are both in our seventies. Do we get tired? Yes, we get bloody tired. There are evenings when either Barbara or I say, "I just can't handle another dinner this week." But we are all here for a limited time. Make the most of it!

The three things you must not take for granted are your health, your family, and your friends. I enjoy meeting new people and making new friends. They add to and enhance our lives and our interest in life. One of my great pleasures is the opportunity I am afforded to meet young people seeking advice. My calendar is frequently full of meetings with students at various inflection points in their lives. On a given day I might meet with somebody who wants to go to college, followed by somebody who just graduated college or who just got an internship. All of these young people help keep me young. Their enthusiasm is infectious. At the same time, I am able to impart my experience.

I suppose there will come a time when this all becomes too much, but until that becomes painfully evident, full speed ahead!

LESSON 18

CONCLUSION

I s life about judgment or about luck? In my experience, it is about luck *and* judgment. In 1962, I was a world-class swimmer in Johannesburg. I was looking to go to the 1964 Olympic Games in Tokyo. In 1962, the International Olympic Committee banned South Africa from the Olympics. This was very bad luck for me.

I immediately decided to apply to business schools in the United States. I applied to four schools and elected to go to Columbia Business School in the city of New York. Good judgment.

On my way to Columbia in 1963, I stopped in Israel for a week to visit my sister. A couple of days after arriving in Tel Aviv, I went to a hotel swimming pool for the afternoon. I sat a couple of feet away from a young girl. We started talking. She was from London and was at the hotel with her parents on vacation. That night, Barbara and I had dinner together.

We had dinner for three consecutive nights before she left to go back to London. Meeting her was good luck.

I followed her to London and spent a couple of months in that city before going to Columbia. Good judgment. Barbara got a job with TWA in London and was posted to New York. Both good judgment and good luck.

I graduated in 1965, and we were married in London in August of that year. My parents and my sister, Gaia, as well as Barbara's family attended the splendid wedding. We have been married fifty-five years; we have two children and six grandchildren. Bad luck followed by good luck followed by good judgment followed by good luck followed by more good judgment. This can only be understood on reflection.

Luck and judgment determine almost all the important decisions we make in life. This doesn't mean that we must take for granted that we will either have much good luck or good judgment. This means that we need to have a plan, a program, a focus, an objective, a career. We cannot have everything that we wish to have, but we can and we must look to the future as well as the present. We all have a propensity to languish. We tend to take things for granted and assume that it will all work out. We may know what we need to do but procrastinate because it means taking a risk, because we're not decisive, or because we don't have the energy—physical or intellectual—to move ahead.

Don't allow yourself to be bullied to accommodate a bully. Even more important, don't you ever be a bully. A bully is not confident. A bully is arrogant. Don't threaten, and don't be

Feldberg grandchildren: Adam, Sarah, Max, Sophia, Danielle, Noa

threatened. Be bold. Take risks. Go to new countries and cities in your late teens or early twenties. Leave home. Leave your family and friends behind you. Go to a new world and explore.

Hopefully your life will be long, productive, and happy. There will be bad moments. You can't plan on everything, but you can have a view of the type of life you want to lead and who your partner will be.

A great life is one in which you are always moving forward. You are looking for variety. You are looking to travel. You are looking to overcome roadblocks. As you move from school to university, from university to a career, from being single to having a partner, you should never leave behind the friends and family you have accumulated over the years.

Keep accumulating friends. A successful life means you still have, at the age of seventy-seven, friends with whom you went to school on another continent and close friends you met only a few years ago. Don't lose friends along the course of your life. Acquire new ones. Bring them all together.

Go through your life giving credit to those who have been helpful, those who have been successful, and those who may fall on hard times. Always try to be generous and agreeable. Keep in mind that we depend on others and that they depend on us.

Finally, at seventy-seven, I have not retired. I can't retire. I feel compelled to be engaged and involved with my career, my service, my children, my grandchildren, my family. I know that I still have some juice—physical energy, intellectual energy, emotional energy, moral energy. I still focus on my health. I exercise every day and am very careful about what I put in my body. Do not run away from life.

I have had the good fortune to have led an interesting life. I grew up under unique circumstances, pursued a career in education and business, and had some fortunate encounters that became foundational to everything that followed. From my days as a boy back in Johannesburg competitively swimming to my present role as a senior advisor at Morgan Stanley, I have always lived life to the fullest, energetically, intensely, and with intention.

I don't expect that everyone reading this book will relate directly to the details of the life stories I have told. Fewer and fewer people have the direct lived experience of growing up under apartheid. Few people have the opportunity to be members of corporate boards, let alone multiple boards. Yet the details, while important to me—these are the stories of my life, after all—are beside the point for the thoughtful reader. Each of these stories turns on a fundamental lesson of a life lived well. No matter who you are and no matter what the circumstances, the lessons at the heart of this book are universal. Pace, self-awareness, calculated risk, recognition of life's fragility, admitting mistakes, confronting injustice, owning up to challenges, generosity of spirit, appreciation of place, social engagement, active leadership, using power responsibly, knowing when to make an extra effort, tending to friendships, engaging in community participation, and maintaining an active life are important values in all domains of life, be they personal or professional. The skills that make one a good corporate board member—namely, responsibility to the investors and organization—are the same if it's the town school board, the PTA, or the Boy Scout troop. The same goes for all of the lessons covered in this book.

In the end there is no finish line. Life is not a race. Life is what happens to us day to day, and it is up to us to live our lives to the fullest and be our best selves. I've tried my best. Sometimes I've succeeded. Other times I haven't. In every case I've done my best to learn and be a better person for it. I hope that you will do the same and make the world a better place.

Portrait of Meyer Feldberg by Barbara Feldberg

EPILOGUE

My wife has been a professional artist for fifty-five years. She has had exhibitions in Cape Town, in Chicago, and in New York. Our favorite galleries are of course those closest to our homes in Manhattan and Vail. Over the years, it has been gratifying that strangers and friends alike have acquired Barbara's paintings.

I am always a bit disappointed when she sells one. Our children and I miss having them hanging at our home or our children's homes. There is, however, an upside to the paintings that she has sold to friends. We still get to see them, just in another setting. Whenever we visit our friends, we find ourselves looking at Barbara's paintings in their dining rooms, foyers, lounges, or studies, and it is a good and warm feeling to know that our friends think so highly of Barbara's work that they hang her art in such prominent places. We recently visited with friends in the country for a long weekend. When we arrived at the house, one of the first things we noticed was a large Barbara Feldberg canvas that looked out over the dining room and outside terrace.

When we are in New York, Barbara goes to her studio pretty much every weekday for six to eight hours. She has sitters, including grandchildren and friends, whom she regards as long-suffering. She's currently working on a painting of me. It's a nude. She won't let anyone see it. She covers it up if anyone walks in while she's working on it. I want to put it in our entrance hall so that it is the first thing you see when you enter our home! This will never happen.